salsas

relishes and dips

salsas
relishes and dips

SILVANA FRANCO

LORENZ BOOKS

Published by Lorenz Books
an imprint of
Anness Publishing Limited
Hermes House, 88-89 Blackfriars Road
London SE1 8HA

This edition distributed in Canada by Raincoast Books
8680 Cambie Street, Vancouver, British Columbia V6P 6M9

ISBN 0-7548-0121-7

A CIP catalogue record for this book
is available from the British Library

Publisher: Joanna Lorenz
Senior Cookery Editor: Linda Fraser
Designer: Brian Weldon
Jacket Design: D.W. Design
Photographer: William Adams-Lingwood
Home Economist: Lucy McKelvie, assisted by Alison Austin

Previously published as part of the *Step-by-Step* cookery series

Printed and bound in China

© Anness Publishing Limited 1997, 1999
3 5 7 9 10 8 6 4 2

MEASUREMENTS
For all recipes, quantities are given in both metric and imperial measures, and,
where appropriate, measures are also given in standard cups and spoons. Follow
one set, but not a mixture, because they are not interchangeable.

CONTENTS

INTRODUCTION

Whether cool and creamy or fiery hot, salsas, relishes and dips are designed to enliven eating. Offer them with plain dishes, such as grilled fish or chops, spoon them into piping-hot baked potatoes, use to top sandwich fillings, or simply serve them with a bowl of tortilla chips. The versatility of these tasty sauces makes them a valuable addition to every meal.

Supermarket shelves are brimming with ready-made salsas and relishes, and chill cabinets are overflowing with daring dips, so there's no doubt that these flavour-savours are fast catching on; but why bother buying the often bland, commercially made varieties when it's so quick and simple – and far tastier – to make them yourself?

Many of these recipes do not involve cooking and are based on fresh fruit and vegetables combined with flavourings such as herbs, garlic and fresh chillies. There is a selection of robust relishes that require a minimum preparation but, with the addition of vinegar and spices, last a few weeks in the fridge – perfect for planning ahead. For those who like it hot, the Fast and Fiery chapter is packed with full-flavoured, no-cook recipes. The page on instant dips also provides a great selection of incredibly speedy dips to present to hungry children or early guests.

Whether you have bags of time to prepare your party or need dips quickly, there's no reason why you can't whip up a few creations of your own. All the recipes are simple to make and they can be adjusted to suit your store cupboard or personal taste. Be adventurous and pair unusual dishes, for example try the minty Aromatic Peach and Cucumber Salsa with traditional roast lamb, or Malted Chocolate and Banana Dip with cocktail-stick-speared strawberries. However you choose to serve it, a little salsa is sure to add a sparkle to your meals.

Fruit

The varying colours, flavours and textures of fruit make them the ideal ingredient for many salsas, relishes and dips.

Bananas
Packed with nutrients and full of flavour, it's worth being sure that the bananas you buy are at their best. Choose fruit that are deep yellow, firm to the touch and without black spots on them.

Melons
There are lots of different melons available depending upon the time of year. Crisp-fleshed watermelons and juicy, orange-fleshed melons, such as Charentais, make super fruity salsas.

Papayas
Also known as paw paw, the papaya is a sweet-fleshed fruit with edible seeds. It is rich in vitamin A and acts as a very good digestive when served at the end of a meal.

Pineapples
Pineapple can be used in both sweet and savoury dishes but must be served when ripe and fresh. Choose fruit that feels firm, with a definite pineapple aroma; a leaf pulled from the centre should come away easily.

Passion fruit
Cut the fruit in half to reveal the succulent, aromatic pulp and edible seeds. Serve with other tropical fruit or with ice cream.

Mangoes
Mango is wonderful for serving fresh in salsas and dips or cooking down into sweet chutney. The ripeness of mango is not determined by colour: to test the fruit, press it gently and the flesh should give slightly when ripe.

Oranges
The juice, flesh and grated rind of oranges are both fragrant and flavoursome. Use them to add a delicious tangy sparkle to sauces, relishes and fruity salsas.

Vegetables

From juicy sweet-fleshed tomatoes to the smooth and creamy-textured avocado – vegetables make an ideal base for, or a colourful crunchy addition to, all sorts of salsas, relishes and dips.

Avocados
The skin and large stone of the avocado are inedible. The flesh, however, can be mashed until smooth and creamy to make a perfect salsa base. Avocado discolours quickly, so brush cut surfaces with lemon juice to preserve them, and use any avocado-based salsa soon after mixing.

Cucumbers
Cool refreshing cucumbers chosen for salsas and crudités must feel firm to the touch. The skin adds texture and fibre, so avoid peeling them.

Onions
Spring onions, red onions, shallots and everyday onions are all frequently used in salsas, relishes and dips. Spring onions and red onions are mild enough to serve raw, while shallots and ordinary onions melt into sweetness when cooked gently over a low heat.

Peppers
Red, yellow and orange peppers have a sweet flavour that is enhanced by roasting and grilling. Green peppers taste fresh and herby and are best sliced, served raw in salads or salsas.

Sweetcorn
If buying fresh corn cobs, choose plump cobs with tightly packed kernels. Remove the papery leaves and silks or husk and boil in plain water (salt toughens the kernels) for 5 minutes, until bright yellow. Lift out of the water, season with salt and smother with butter.

Tomatoes
The most essential salsa ingredient – opt for plump, firm-fleshed tomatoes that are a good shade of red. Though available all year, tomatoes are at their best in summer, simply because they are often grown in hothouses during winter months and are then not only expensive but also lacking in flavour.

Fresh Flavourings

An essential element of even the most basic of
salsas, at least one fresh flavouring is found in
just about every recipe in this book.

Lemons
Although lemons
are not suitable for
eating as a dessert fruit,
the tang offered by the
juice of a lemon is a valuable
addition to many dishes. Its
acid content also makes
lemon juice useful for
preventing the discoloration
of fruit and vegetables, such
as avocado and banana.

Garlic
Garlic is at the heart of
Mediterranean cuisine as a
valuable flavouring with
medicinal properties. When
raw, it is best used in small
amounts since its pungent
flavour and aroma go a long
way; on cooking, however, it
becomes mellow and sweet
and makes a delicious
addition to salsas and dips.
Either chop or crush peeled
cloves and then fry the garlic
briefly over a low heat in a
little olive oil, or place
unpeeled cloves in a roasting
tin and bake them in the
oven until tender before
peeling and mashing.

Chillies
Available in countless shapes,
sizes and varying shades of
red and green, chillies can be
fairly mild or exceedingly hot.
It is often difficult to tell the
difference – one rule that
does seem to apply to most
types, is that the thinner the
skin, the hotter the chilli. If
you have sensitive skin, wear
gloves when handling them.
In any case, always wash your
hands thoroughly after
handling them.

Limes
Sister to the lemon, the
lime has a slightly more sour
flavour that is often
associated with the food of
Southeast Asia. It can be used
to add a sharp tang to salsas
and dips. If using in place of
lemon juice, reduce the
quantity slightly. Grated lime
rind can also used as a
colourful, tart flavouring.

Root ginger
Peeled and then thinly sliced,
chopped, shredded or grated,
fresh root ginger can be used
to enhance all manner of
salsas, dips and relishes with
its warming, spicy flavour.

Herbs

Colourful fresh herbs make a flavourful addition to a wide variety of salsas, relishes and dips – don't chop them too finely, but leave them roughly chopped for maximum flavour.

Basil
Sweet basil (above) is used mainly in savoury dishes, often paired with tomatoes. Opal basil (right) is a dark purple variety.

Parsley
Parsley has a mild flavour and fragrance that makes it suitable for use in large quantities in salsas and dips. Both the curly-leafed variety and the more flavoursome continental-style flat-leaf parsley (right) are available.

Chives
This classic French herb with a delicate onion flavour is best served raw. Snip it over chilled salsas or dips for a pretty garnish.

Mint
We often reserve mint for lamb or peas, but in fact it can be used very successfully to liven up many sauces and salsas in a similar way to the more experimental uses for basil and parsley. There are many different varieties of mint, including peppermint, spearmint and apple mint.

Coriander
Fresh coriander is one of the most useful herbs for salsa making. Its flavour is well matched by lime and chillies, and it is also good in any tomato-based salsa, dip or relish. The dried seed of this herb is a warm fragrant spice that is often used in Middle-Eastern and Asian cookery.

Spices

Strong-flavoured and aromatic, whole or ground, spices are ideal for pepping up a salsa, relish or dip.

Cayenne
This is made from whole hot chillies, so it is extremely powerful and should be used sparingly (1).

Chilli flakes
Dried chilli flakes are handy for sprinkling into sauces and relishes. They are very hot, so handle them with care (2).

Cinnamon
Cinnamon can be bought either ground or as sticks of bark, which cannot be eaten and have to be removed from the dish after their flavour has been imparted (4).

Cumin seeds
Often associated with Asian and North African cookery, cumin can be bought ground or as small, slender seeds. If using the seeds whole, first roast or dry-fry them to bring out their flavour (3).

Ground ginger
Ground ginger is a useful standby and makes a spicy addition to cooked relishes (5).

Saffron
The most precious spice of all, saffron is prepared from crocus stamens. The best is reputed to come from Spain. Use either saffron threads or the ready-ground powder (6).

Storecupboard Sauces

The wide range of storecupboard sauces and condiments means that speedy, simple dips and salsas are never very far away. Here are some of the most useful standbys.

Angostura
Angostura aromatic bitters are a special blend of vegetable spices; the product is not actually made from the angostura bark after which it is named. Often used in drinks and cocktails, bitters also add an interesting twist to salsas and dips (6).

Coconut cream
Coconut cream is a thick, but pouring, commercially made sauce which comes in handy-size cartons and is often used in Thai-style curries (8).

Curry pastes
Curry pastes are made from oils and Indian spices. They have already been cooked, so can be stirred into sauces without introducing the harshness of raw curry powder. Red and green Thai curry pastes are made with chillies, garlic and lemon grass – they are very concentrated and have a superb flavour (10).

Hoisin sauce
Hoisin is a rich, thick sauce with a sweet and savoury flavour. It is a classic accompaniment for Chinese crispy duck. Readily available alongside other Oriental ingredients in supermarkets, it can be stirred into passata or creamed tomatoes to make a delicious savoury dip (7).

Horseradish sauce
Hot and peppery horseradish sauce is not just for roast beef: stir it into creamy or tomato bases to make a pleasing dip (9).

Liquid smoke marinade
Now appearing in larger supermarkets and specialist food stores, Liquid smoke is intended for marinating meats prior to grilling, but a teaspoonful adds a delicious flavour to tomato-based salsas and relishes (11).

Mayonnaise
Ready-made mayonnaise makes a fantastic base for creamy dips. It can be prepared at home, in which case it must be chilled and used promptly (12).

Mustard
There are many varieties of mustard, all of which are useful for whisking into dressings, dips and sauces. Wholegrain mustard has a mild flavour and a good texture, and it tastes great stirred into creamy bases such as Greek yogurt or mayonnaise (13).

Soy sauce
Sweet and salty soy sauce is made from fermented soy beans and roasted wheat or barley. It is matured in wooden casks for months before being filtered (5).

Tabasco sauce
Tabasco sauce has a distinctive aroma and hot chilli flavour. Green Tabasco, made from jalapeño chillies, has a milder flavour than the original red sauce and can be used more liberally (4).

Vinegar
Vinegar is made from soured alcohol such as wine or cider. Wine vinegar (3) can be used to make simple salad dressings where its sharp acidic flavour is balanced by oil. As a flavouring for salsas and dips the best to use is the deliciously sweet-sour balsamic vinegar (2), which originates from Modena in Northern Italy and is matured in wooden casks.

Worcestershire sauce
Cooked to a secret recipe, Worcestershire sauce contains garlic, shallots, chillies, anchovies, malt vinegar and other ingredients. It is a full-bodied savoury flavouring for marinades and sauces (1).

Instant Dips

Whip up some speedy dips for an impromptu cocktail party or to impress unexpected guests with the help of storecupboard classics, such as mayonnaise, sun-dried tomatoes and soy sauce.

Creamy black olive dip

To make a great dip for bread sticks, stir a little black olive paste into a carton of extra thick double cream until smooth and well blended. Add salt and freshly ground black pepper and a squeeze of fresh lemon juice to taste. Serve chilled. For a low-calorie version, substitute low-fat or Greek-style natural yogurt for the cream.

Crème fraîche or soured cream with spring onions

Finely chop a bunch of spring onions and stir into a carton of crème fraîche or soured cream. Add a dash of chilli sauce, a squeeze of fresh lime juice and a little salt and freshly ground black pepper to taste. Serve with tortilla chips or alongside a spicy guacamole.

Greek-style yogurt and grainy mustard dip

Mix a small carton of creamy Greek-style yogurt with one or two teaspoons of wholegrain mustard. Serve with grissini or crudités.

Herby mayonnaise

Liven up ready-made French-style mayonnaise with a handful of chopped fresh herbs – try flat-leaf parsley, basil, dill or tarragon. Season to taste with plenty of freshly ground black pepper and serve with crisp carrot and cucumber batons.

Passata and horseradish dip

Bring a little tang to a small carton or bottle of passata (sieved tomatoes) by adding some horseradish sauce or a teaspoon or two of creamed horseradish. Add salt and pepper to taste and serve with spicy tortilla chips.

Pesto dip

For a simple, speedy Italian-style dip, stir a tablespoon of ready-made red or green pesto into a carton of soured cream. Serve with crisp crudités or wedges of oven-roasted Mediterranean vegetables, such as peppers, courgettes and onions.

Soft cheese and chive dip

Mix a tub of skimmed milk soft cheese with two or three tablespoons of snipped fresh chives and season to taste with salt and plenty of black pepper. If the dip is a little too thick, stir in a spoonful or two of milk to soften it.

Spiced yogurt dip

To make a speedy Indian-style dip, stir a little mild or hot and spicy curry paste into a carton of natural yogurt. Add a finely chopped apple or a spoonful or two of mango chutney and serve with crisp poppadoms.

Yogurt and sun-dried tomato dip

Stir one or two tablespoons of sun-dried tomato paste into a carton of Greek-style yogurt. Season to taste with salt and freshly ground black pepper. Serve with small triangles of crisp toasted pitta bread or salted crisps. Alternatively use soured cream in place of the yogurt.

Creamy black
olive dip

Crème fraîche with
spring onions

Yogurt and
sun-dried tomato dip

Herby
mayonnaise

Greek-style
yogurt and grainy
mustard dip

Sour
and chive
dip

Spiced yogurt dip

Pesto dip

horseradish dip

Serving Suggestions

There are many ways to serve salsas, relishes and dips: they can be spooned on to the side, or over the top, of fish, chicken or meat dishes, used as a sandwich filling or topping, or served with anti-pasti or cheese. One of the fun ways to serve them is with a selection of titbits for dipping.

Bread sticks
Choose crunchy Italian-style grissini bread sticks for thick and creamy dips and salsas. To serve them, either pile the bread sticks on to a plate or in a large bowl, or stand them in a tall glass or jug.

Cheese straws
These are ideal for dipping and dunking. You can buy cheese straws ready-made, but they are very easy to make at home. Simply roll out a small packet of puff pastry thinly and cut it into strips. Lightly brush the strips with beaten egg and sprinkle with a little grated cheese. (Twist the strips first, if you like.) Chill for 10 minutes, then bake them at 180°C/350°F/Gas 4 for 15–20 minutes or until puffed and golden. Cool on a wire rack before serving.

Corn chips
These crisp ready-made Mexican-style snacks are now widely available in delicatessens and supermarkets. Choose cheese-flavoured corn chips for creamy dips and the plain variety for spicier tomato-based salsas. Look out for tasty blue corn chips in speciality shops and food halls.

Fruit crudités
These make the perfect accompaniment to sweet dips. Cut chunks of peach, nectarine, pear, banana or apple and arrange on a platter with whole or halved strawberries, segments of oranges, plums, sharon fruit or not-too-ripe figs.

Potato crisps
Salted crisps, either the plain variety or one of the many flavours, are a popular storecupboard standby and make a great accompaniment to absolutely any dip. Choose the thicker ones for chunky or very thick dips and only serve light, creamy dips with the more fragile varieties.

Tortilla chips
The classic accompaniment to chilled tomato salsa, tortilla chips are now available in a variety of flavours. Serve the fiery chips with creamy dips and the cool ones with robust salsas or relishes.

Vegetable crisps
There are some brands of vegetable crisps available to buy ready-made, but they are also easy to make at home. Several different vegetables work well, try sweet potato, beetroot, carrot, parsnip or, of course, potato. Peel the vegetables, slice them wafer-thin with a mandoline or swivel-style vegetable peeler, then deep fry the slices in hot vegetable oil and season them with plenty of salt and a little chilli powder, paprika or cayenne pepper.

Vegetable crudités
Chunks, sticks or wedges of fresh raw vegetables make brilliant scoops for all manner of dips and salsas. Try sticks of carrot, celery and cucumber; cut thin strips of more than one colour of pepper; or trim small florets of cauliflower or broccoli. To make wedges or "scoops", cut small peppers lengthways into thin wedges, trim celery into short lengths, or cut 5 cm/2 in pieces of cucumber into six lengthways and remove the seeds. Crisp chicory leaves and the small central leaves from cos or Little Gem lettuces also make delicious crudités.

Cheese straws and
bread sticks

Fruit
crudités

Vegetable
crudités

Corn chips

Tortilla chips

Vegetable crisps

Potato crisps

TECHNIQUES

Preparing Chillies

The hottest chillies need very careful handling – just follow these simple steps. If you do touch chillies, wash your hands thoroughly.

1 To remove the skin from habanero chillies, skewer the chillies, one at a time, on a metal fork and hold over a gas flame for 2–3 minutes, turning the chilli until the skin blackens and blisters.

2 Leave the chillies to cool for a few minutes, then use a clean dish towel to rub off the skins.

3 Try not to touch the chillies with your bare hands; use a fork to hold them and slice them open with a sharp knife.

4 Even the less hot varieties of chillies can be fairly fiery. To reduce the heat, cut the chillies in half and scrape out the seeds using the tip of a knife.

Peeling Peppers

Peppers are delicious added raw to salads. However, roasting them first softens the flesh and gives them a delicious warm flavour.

1 Preheat the grill to medium. Place the peppers on a baking sheet and grill for 8–12 minutes, turning regularly, until the skins have blackened and blistered.

2 Place the peppers in a bowl and cover with a clean dish towel. Leave for 5 minutes so the steam helps to lift the skin away from the flesh.

3 When the peppers are cool enough to handle, pierce a hole in the bottom of each one and gently squeeze out the juices into a bowl.

4 Peel off and discard the skins from the peppers and then chop or slice as required in recipes.

Preparing Tomatoes

Flame-skinning tomatoes is the simplest and quickest method.

1 Skewer one tomato at a time on a metal fork and hold in a gas flame for 1–2 minutes, turning it until the skin splits and wrinkles.

2 Leave the tomatoes until cool enough to handle, then slip off and discard the skins.

3 Halve the tomatoes, then scoop out the seeds using a teaspoon.

4 Finely chop the tomatoes using a small sharp knife and use as required.

Cook's Tip
If you don't have a gas cooker, simply place the tomatoes in a bowl of boiling water for 30–60 seconds, until the skin splits. Rinse the tomatoes under cold water, then peel.

Preparing Cucumber

Cucumber can be cut into strips and then softened for use in delicate salsas by salting.

1 Trim off the ends from the cucumber and cut it into 2.5 cm/1 in lengths, then slice each piece lengthways into thin strips.

2 Place the cucumber slices in a colander and sprinkle with 5 ml/1 tsp salt. Leave for 5 minutes until wilted.

3 Wash the cucumber slices well under cold running water, then drain and pat them dry with kitchen paper.

Preparing Mangoes

Removing the stone and skin from a mango can be done in three easy steps.

Peeling a Pineapple

Try this clever all-in-one way of removing the peel from a fresh pineapple.

1 Holding the mango upright on a chopping board, use a large knife to slice the flesh away from either side of the large flat stone in two pieces. Using a smaller knife, carefully trim away the flesh still clinging to the stone

2 Score the flesh of the mango halves deeply, taking care to avoid cutting through the skin; make parallel incisions about 1 cm/½ in apart, then turn the mango half and cut lines in the opposite direction.

1 Holding the pineapple in one hand on a board, cut off the leafy top using a large sharp knife.

3 Carefully turn the skin inside out so that the flesh stands out like hedgehog spikes. Slice the diced flesh away from the skin.

2 Cutting at a 45° angle, make an incision in the pineapple skin, following the natural diagonal line of the eyes. When you reach the end of the line, turn the pineapple over and cut the other side of the line of eyes in the same way. Pull off the strip of skin.

3 Continue cutting the skin of the pineapple in the same way until it is completely peeled, then slice or chop as required in recipes.

Segmenting Oranges

Orange segments without any skin are useful for adding to salsas or serving alongside sweet dips.

Making Mayonnaise

Home-made mayonnaise tastes wonderful and is very quick and simple to prepare.

1 Slice the bottom off the orange so that it will stand firmly on a chopping board. Using a sharp knife, remove the peel by slicing from the top to the bottom of the orange.

2 Hold the orange in one hand over a bowl. Slice towards the middle of the fruit, to one side of the segment, and then gently twist the knife to ease the segment away from the membrane and out of the orange. Repeat to remove all of the segments. Squeeze any juice from the remaining membrane into the bowl.

1 Place the egg yolks and lemon juice in a food processor or blender and process them briefly until lightly blended.

2 Pour the oil into a jug, then with the machine running pour in the oil in a slow, steady stream.

Preparing Avocados

Removing the flesh from avocados is easy to do.

1 Cut around the avocado, twist to separate the halves, remove the stone, then scoop out the flesh into a bowl.

2 Mash the flesh well with a fork or a potato masher, or tip out on to a board and chop finely using a large knife.

3 Once half the oil has been added, add the remaining oil more quickly. Continue processing until the mayonnaise is thick and creamy, add a little lemon juice and season with salt and pepper to taste.

Mango and Radish Salsa

The sweet flavour and juicy texture of mango in this salsa is contrasted very well by the hot and crunchy radishes. Simply serve with plain grilled fish or chicken.

Serves 4

INGREDIENTS
1 large, ripe mango
12 radishes
juice of 1 lemon
45 ml/3 tbsp olive oil
red Tabasco sauce, to taste
45 ml/3 tbsp chopped fresh
   coriander
5 ml/1 tsp pink peppercorns
salt

TO SERVE
lettuce leaves
watercress sprigs
slices of seeded bread

mango   radishes

olive   lemon   red
oil   juice   Tabasco
          sauce

coriander   pink
       peppercorns

VARIATION
Try using papaya in place of the mango in this salsa.

1 Holding the mango upright on a chopping board, use a large knife to slice the flesh away from either side of the large flat stone in two pieces. Using a smaller knife, carefully trim away any flesh still clinging to the top and bottom of the stone.

2 Score the flesh of the mango halves deeply, taking care to avoid cutting through the skin: make parallel incisions about 1 cm/½ in apart; turn and cut lines in the opposite direction. Carefully turn the skin inside out so the flesh stands out like hedgehog spikes. Slice the diced flesh away from the skin.

3 Trim the radishes, discarding the root tails and leaves. Coarsely grate the radishes or dice them finely and place in a bowl with the mango cubes.

4 Stir the lemon juice and olive oil with salt and a few drops of Tabasco sauce to taste, then stir in the chopped coriander.

5 Coarsely crush the pink peppercorns in a pestle and mortar or place them on a chopping board and flatten them with the heel of a heavy-bladed knife. Stir into the lemon oil.

6 Toss the radishes and mango, pour in the dressing and toss again. Chill for up to 2 hours before serving.

Guacamole

Nachos or tortilla chips are the perfect accompaniment for this classic Mexican dip.

Serves 4

INGREDIENTS
2 ripe avocados
2 red chillies, seeded
1 garlic clove
1 shallot
30 ml/2 tbsp olive oil, plus extra
    to serve
juice of 1 lemon
salt
flat-leaf parsley leaves, to garnish

avocados

red chillies

shallot

olive oil

garlic

flat-leaf parsley

lemon juice

1 Halve the avocados, remove their stones and, using a spoon, scoop out their flesh into a bowl.

2 Mash the flesh well with a potato masher or a large fork.

3 Finely chop the chillies, garlic and shallot, then stir into the mashed avocado with the olive oil and lemon juice. Add salt to taste.

4 Spoon the mixture into a small serving bowl. Drizzle over a little olive oil and scatter with a few flat-leaf parsley leaves. Serve immediately.

VARIATION

Make a completely smooth guacamole by whizzing the ingredients in a blender or food processor. For a chunkier version, add a diced tomato or red pepper.

Saucy Tomato Dip

This versatile dip is delicious served with absolutely anything and can be made up to 24 hours in advance.

Serves 4

INGREDIENTS
1 shallot
2 garlic cloves
handful of fresh basil leaves, plus
    extra, to garnish
500 g/1¼ lb ripe tomatoes
30 ml/2 tbsp olive oil
2 green chillies
salt and pepper

shallot

garlic

basil

tomatoes

green chillies

olive oil

1 Peel and halve the shallot and garlic cloves. Place in a blender or food processor with the basil leaves, then process the ingredients until they are very finely chopped.

2 Halve the tomatoes and add to the shallot mixture. Pulse the power until the mixture is well blended and the tomatoes are finely chopped.

3 With the motor still running, slowly pour in the olive oil. Add salt and pepper to taste.

4 Halve the chillies lengthways and remove their seeds. Finely slice them across into tiny strips and stir them into the tomato mixture. Serve at room temperature. Garnish with a few torn basil leaves.

COOK'S TIP
This dip is best made with full-flavoured sun-ripened tomatoes. In winter, use a drained 400 g/14 oz can of plum tomatoes.

Salsa Verde

There are many versions of this classic green salsa. Serve this one with creamy mashed potatoes or drizzled over chargrilled squid.

Serves 4

INGREDIENTS
2–4 green chillies
8 spring onions
2 garlic cloves
50 g/2 oz salted capers
fresh tarragon sprig
bunch of fresh parsley
grated rind and juice of 1 lime
juice of 1 lemon
90 ml/6 tbsp olive oil
about 15 ml/1 tbsp green Tabasco
   sauce, to taste
black pepper

chillies

spring onions

tarragon

garlic

capers

lime juice and grated lime rind

parsley

lemon juice

olive oil

green Tabasco sauce

VARIATION

If you can find only capers pickled in vinegar, they can be used for this salsa but must be rinsed well in cold water first.

1 Halve the chillies and remove their seeds. Trim the spring onions and halve the garlic, then place in a food processor. Pulse the power briefly until all the ingredients are roughly chopped.

2 Use your fingertips to rub the excess salt off the capers but do not rinse them (see Variation, below). Add the capers, tarragon and parsley to the food processor and pulse again until they are quite finely chopped.

3 Transfer the mixture to a small bowl. Stir in the lime rind and juice, lemon juice and olive oil. Stir the mixture lightly so the citrus juice and oil do not emulsify.

4 Add green Tabasco and black pepper to taste. Chill until ready to serve but do not prepare more than 8 hours in advance.

Avocado and Red Pepper Salsa

This simple salsa is a fire-and-ice mixture of hot chilli and cooling avocado. Serve corn chips and crisps for dipping.

Serves 4

INGREDIENTS
2 ripe avocados
1 red onion
1 red pepper
4 green chillies
30 ml/2 tbsp chopped fresh
  coriander
30 ml/2 tbsp sunflower oil
juice of 1 lemon
salt and pepper

avocados
red onion
red pepper
green chillies
coriander
sunflower oil   lemon juice

COOK'S TIP

The cut surface of avocados discolour very quickly, so if you plan to prepare this salsa in advance, make sure the avocados are coated with fresh lemon juice to help prevent discoloration.

1 Halve and stone the avocados. Scoop out and finely dice the flesh. Finely chop the red onion.

2 Slice the top off the pepper and pull out the central core. Shake out any remaining seeds. Cut the pepper into thin strips and then into dice.

3 Halve the chillies, remove their seeds and finely chop them. Mix the chillies, coriander, oil, lemon and salt and pepper to taste.

4 Place the avocado, red onion and pepper in a bowl. Pour in the chilli and coriander dressing and toss the mixture well. Serve immediately.

Fiery Citrus Salsa

This very unusual salsa makes a fantastic marinade for shellfish and it is also delicious drizzled over barbecued meat.

Serves 4

INGREDIENTS
1 orange
1 green apple
2 fresh red chillies
1 garlic clove
8 fresh mint leaves
juice of 1 lemon
salt and pepper

orange   *apple*

red chillies   *garlic*

mint   *lemon juice*

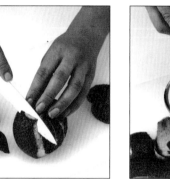

1 Slice the bottom off the orange so that it will stand firmly on a chopping board. Using a sharp knife, remove the peel by slicing from the top to the bottom of the orange.

2 Hold the orange in one hand over a bowl. Slice towards the middle of the fruit, to one side of a segment, and then gently twist the knife to ease the segment away from the membrane and out of the orange. Repeat to remove all the segments. Squeeze any juice from the remaining membrane into the bowl.

3 Peel the apple, slice it into wedges and remove the core.

4 Halve the chillies and remove their seeds, then place them in a blender or food processor with the orange segments and juice, apple wedges, garlic and fresh mint.

5 Process until smooth. Then, with the motor running, pour in the lemon juice.

6 Season to taste with a little salt and pepper. Pour into a bowl or small jug and serve immediately.

VARIATION

If you're feeling really fiery, don't seed the chillies! They will make the salsa particularly hot and fierce.

Bloody Mary Relish

Serve this perfect party salsa with sticks of crunchy cucumber or, on a really special occasion, with freshly shucked oysters.

Serves 2

INGREDIENTS
4 ripe tomatoes
1 celery stalk
1 garlic clove
2 spring onions
45 ml/3 tbsp tomato juice
Worcestershire sauce, to taste
red Tabasco sauce, to taste
10 ml/2 tsp horseradish sauce
15 ml/1 tbsp vodka
juice of 1 lemon
salt and pepper

1 Halve the tomatoes, celery and garlic. Trim the spring onions.

tomatoes

celery

garlic

spring onions

tomato juice

red Tabasco sauce

vodka

Worcestershire sauce

horseradish sauce

lemon juice

2 Process the vegetables in a blender or food processor until very finely chopped, then transfer them to a bowl.

VARIATION
Whizz 1–2 fresh seeded, red chillies with the tomatoes instead of adding Tabasco sauce.

3 Stir in the tomato juice and add a few drops of Worcestershire sauce and Tabasco to taste.

4 Stir in the horseradish sauce, vodka and lemon juice. Add salt and freshly ground black pepper, to taste.

Piquant Pineapple Relish

This fruity sweet-and-sour relish is excellent served with grilled chicken or bacon.

Serves 4

INGREDIENTS
400 g/14 oz can crushed pineapple
  in natural juice
30 ml/2 tbsp light muscovado sugar
30 ml/2 tbsp wine vinegar
1 garlic clove
4 spring onions
2 red chillies
10 fresh basil leaves
salt and pepper

pineapple   *muscovado sugar*

garlic   *wine vinegar*

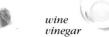

spring onions

red chillies   *basil*

1 Drain the pineapple and reserve 60 ml/4 tbsp of the juice.

2 Place the juice in a small saucepan with the sugar and vinegar, then heat gently, stirring, until the sugar dissolves. Remove from the heat and add salt and pepper to taste.

VARIATION

This relish tastes extra special when made with fresh pineapple – substitute the juice of a freshly squeezed orange for the canned juice.

3 Finely chop the garlic and spring onions. Halve the chillies, remove their seeds and finely chop them. Finely shred the basil leaves.

4 Place the pineapple, garlic, spring onions and chillies in a bowl. Mix well and pour in the sauce. Allow to cool for 5 minutes, then stir in the basil.

Chunky Cherry Tomato Salsa

Succulent cherry tomatoes and refreshing cucumber form the base of this delicious dill-seasoned salsa.

Serves 4

INGREDIENTS
1 ridge cucumber
5 ml/1 tsp sea salt
500 g/1¼ lb cherry tomatoes
1 garlic clove
1 lemon
45 ml/3 tbsp chilli oil
2.5 ml/½ tsp dried chilli flakes
30 ml/2 tbsp chopped fresh dill
salt and pepper

ridge cucumber   *cherry tomatoes*

chilli flakes

chilli oil

fresh dill

lemon   *garlic*

1 Trim the ends off the cucumber and cut it into 2.5 cm/1 in lengths, then cut each piece lengthways into thin slices.

2 Arrange the cucumber slices in a colander and sprinkle them with the sea salt. Leave for 5 minutes until the cucumber has wilted.

3 Wash the cucumber slices well under cold water and pat them dry with kitchen paper.

4 Quarter the cherry tomatoes and place in a bowl with the wilted cucumber. Finely chop the garlic.

5 Grate the lemon rind finely and place in a small jug with the juice from the lemon, the chilli oil, chilli flakes, dill and garlic. Add salt and pepper to taste, and whisk with a fork.

VARIATION
Try flavouring this salsa with other fragrant herbs, such as tarragon, coriander or even mint.

6 Pour the chilli oil dressing over the tomato and cucumber and toss well. Leave to marinate at room temperature for at least 2 hours before serving.

Double Chilli Salsa

This is a scorchingly hot salsa for only the very brave! Spread it sparingly on to cooked meats and burgers.

Serves 4–6

INGREDIENTS
6 habanero chillies or Scotch
   bonnets
2 ripe tomatoes
4 standard green jalapeño chillies
30 ml/2 tbsp chopped fresh parsley
30 ml/2 tbsp olive oil
15 ml/1 tbsp balsamic or sherry
   vinegar
salt

*habanero
chillies*

tomatoes

*jalapeño
chillies*

parsley

olive oil

*balsamic
or sherry
vinegar*

1 Skewer an habanero or Scotch bonnet chilli on a metal fork and hold it in a gas flame for 2–3 minutes, turning the chilli until the skin blackens and blisters. Repeat with all the chillies, then set aside.

2 Skewer the tomatoes one at a time and hold in the flame for 1–2 minutes, until the skin splits and wrinkles. Slip off the skins, halve the tomatoes, then use a teaspoon to scoop out and discard the seeds. Chop the flesh very finely.

3 Use a clean dish towel to rub the skins off the chillies.

4 Try not to touch the chillies with your bare hands: use a fork to hold them and slice them open with a sharp knife. Scrape out and discard the seeds, then finely chop the flesh.

5 Halve the jalapeño chillies, remove their seeds and finely slice them widthways into tiny strips. Mix together both types of chillies, the tomatoes and chopped parsley.

6 Mix the olive oil, vinegar and a little salt, pour this over the salsa and cover the dish. Chill for up to 3 days.

VARIATION
Habanero chillies, or Scotch bonnets, are among the hottest fresh chillies available. You may prefer to tone down the heat of this salsa by using a milder variety.

Satay Sauce

There are many versions of this tasty peanut sauce. This one is very speedy and it tastes delicious drizzled over grilled or barbecued skewers of chicken. For parties, spear chunks of chicken with cocktail sticks and arrange around a bowl of warm sauce.

Serves 4

INGREDIENTS
200 ml/7 fl oz/scant 1 cup
  coconut cream
60 ml/4 tbsp crunchy peanut butter
5 ml/1 tsp Worcestershire sauce
red Tabasco sauce, to taste
fresh coconut, to garnish (optional)

coconut cream

peanut butter

Worcestershire sauce

red Tabasco sauce

coconut

COOK'S TIP

Thick coconut milk can be substituted for coconut cream; coconut milk is usually packed in 400 g/14 oz cans, but take care to buy an unsweetened variety for this recipe.

1 Pour the coconut cream into a small saucepan and heat it gently over a low heat for about 2 minutes.

2 Add the peanut butter and stir vigorously until it is blended into the coconut cream. Continue to heat until the mixture is warm but not boiling.

3 Add the Worcestershire sauce and a dash of Tabasco to taste. Pour into a serving bowl.

4 Use a potato peeler to shave thin strips from a piece of fresh coconut, if using. Scatter the coconut over the sauce and serve immediately.

Feta and Olive Salsa

The salty flavour of the feta and olives in this chunky salsa is balanced by the bitter-tasting radicchio.

Serves 4

INGREDIENTS
1 head of radicchio
250 g/9 oz feta cheese
150 g/5 oz black olives, halved and
    stoned
1 garlic clove
1 red chilli, seeded
45 ml/3 tbsp chopped fresh parsley
30 ml/2 tbsp olive oil
15 ml/1 tbsp balsamic vinegar
sea salt

radicchio

feta cheese

black olives

garlic

red chilli

parsley

olive oil

balsamic vinegar

1 Separate the radicchio leaves and rinse them well in cold water. Roughly tear the leaves into small pieces.

2 Cut or break the feta into small cubes. Place the radicchio in a bowl with the feta and olive halves and toss well to mix together.

COOK'S TIP
Choose unpitted olives such as Kalamata for this salsa – they tend to have a stronger flavour and more interesting texture than the mild, pitted varieties.

3 Finely chop the garlic and chilli, and sprinkle over the salsa with the chopped parsley, olive oil, balsamic vinegar and sea salt to taste.

4 Mix together well, then transfer the salsa to a serving bowl and serve at room temperature.

Chilli Bean Dip

This creamy bean dip is best served warm with triangles of grilled pitta bread or a bowl of crunchy tortilla chips.

Serves 4

INGREDIENTS
2 garlic cloves
1 onion
2 green chillies
30 ml/2 tbsp vegetable oil
5–10 ml/1–2 tsp hot chilli powder
400 g/14 oz can kidney beans
75 g/3 oz mature Cheddar
  cheese, grated
1 red chilli, seeded
salt and pepper

garlic

green chillies

onion

vegetable oil

chilli powder

kidney beans

Cheddar cheese

red chilli

COOK'S TIP

For a dip with a coarser texture, do not purée the beans, instead mash them with a potato masher.

1 Finely chop the garlic and onion. Seed and finely chop the green chillies.

2 Heat the oil in a large sauté pan or deep frying pan and add the garlic, onion, green chillies and chilli powder. Cook gently for 5 minutes, stirring regularly, until the onions are softened and transparent, but not browned.

3 Drain the kidney beans, reserving the liquor. Blend all but 30 ml/2 tbsp of the beans to a purée in a food processor.

4 Add the puréed beans to the pan with 30–45 ml/2–3 tbsp of the reserved liquor. Heat gently, stirring to mix well.

5 Stir in the whole beans and the Cheddar cheese. Cook gently for about 2–3 minutes, stirring until the cheese melts. Add salt and pepper to taste.

6 Cut the red chilli into tiny strips. Spoon the dip into four individual serving bowls and scatter the chilli strips over the top. Serve warm.

Basil and Lemon Mayonnaise

This dip is based on fresh mayonnaise flavoured with lemon juice and two types of basil. Serve with salads, baked potatoes or as a delicious dip for French fries.

Serves 4

INGREDIENTS
2 size 1 egg yolks
15 ml/1 tbsp lemon juice
150 ml/¼ pint/⅔ cup olive oil
150 ml/¼ pint/⅔ cup sunflower oil
4 garlic cloves
handful of green basil leaves
handful of opal basil leaves
salt and pepper

egg yolks

lemon juice

garlic

olive oil

sunflower oil

green basil

opal basil

COOK'S TIP
Make sure all the ingredients are at room temperature before you start to help prevent the mixture from curdling.

1 Place the egg yolks and lemon juice in a blender or food processor and process them briefly until lightly blended.

2 In a jug, stir together both oils. With the machine running, pour in the oil very slowly, a little at a time.

3 Once half of the oil has been added, the remaining oil can be incorporated more quickly. Continue processing to form a thick, creamy mayonnaise.

4 Peel and crush the garlic cloves. Alternatively, place them on a chopping board and sprinkle with salt, then flatten them with the heel of a heavy-bladed knife and chop the flesh. Flatten the garlic again to make a coarse purée.

5 Tear both types of basil into small pieces and stir into the mayonnaise with the crushed garlic.

6 Add salt and pepper to taste, then transfer the dip to a serving dish. Cover and chill until ready to serve.

Hummus

This nutritious dip can be served with vegetable crudités or packed into salad-filled pitta, but it is best spread thickly on hot buttered toast.

Serves 4

INGREDIENTS
400 g/14 oz can chick-peas,
  drained
2 garlic cloves
30 ml/2 tbsp tahini or smooth
  peanut butter
60 ml/4 tbsp olive oil
juice of 1 lemon
2.5 ml/½ tsp cayenne pepper
15 ml/1 tbsp sesame seeds
sea salt

garlic

chick-peas   *sea salt*

olive oil

tahini   *lemon juice*

cayenne pepper   *sesame seeds*

COOK'S TIP
Tahini is a thick smooth and oily paste made from sesame seeds. It is available from health-food shops and large supermarkets. Tahini is a classic ingredient in hummus, this Middle-Eastern dip; peanut butter would not be used in a traditional recipe but it is a useful substitute.

1 Rinse the chick-peas well and place in a blender or food processor with the garlic and a good pinch of sea salt. Process until very finely chopped.

2 Add the tahini or peanut butter and process until fairly smooth. With the motor still running, slowly pour in the oil and lemon juice.

3 Stir in the cayenne pepper and add more salt, to taste. If the mixture is too thick, stir in a little cold water. Transfer the purée to a serving bowl.

4 Heat a small non-stick pan and add the sesame seeds. Cook for 2–3 minutes, shaking the pan, until the seeds are golden. Allow to cool, then sprinkle over the purée.

Melting Cheese Dip

This is a classic fondue in true Swiss style. It should be served with cubes of crusty, day-old bread, but it is also good with chunks of spicy, cured sausage such as chorizo.

Serves 2

INGREDIENTS
1 garlic clove, finely chopped
150 ml/¼ pint/⅔ cup dry white wine
150 g/5 oz Gruyère cheese
5 ml/1 tsp cornflour
15 ml/1 tbsp Kirsch
salt and pepper

white wine

garlic

Gruyère cheese

cornflour

Kirsch

1 Place the garlic and wine in a small saucepan and bring gently to the boil. Simmer for 3–4 minutes.

2 Coarsely grate the cheese and stir it into the wine. Continue to stir as the cheese melts.

COOK'S TIP
Gruyère is a tasty cheese that melts incredibly well. Don't substitute other cheeses.

3 Blend the cornflour to a smooth paste with the Kirsch and pour into the pan, stirring. Bring to the boil, stirring continuously, until the sauce is smooth and thickened.

4 Add salt and pepper to taste. Serve immediately or, better still, transfer to a fondue pan and place over a spirit burner to keep it hot. Garnish with black pepper.

Lemon and Coconut Dhal

A warm spicy dish, this can be served either as a dip with poppadoms or as a main-meal accompaniment.

Serves 8

INGREDIENTS
5 cm/2 in piece root ginger
1 onion
2 garlic cloves
2 small red chillies, seeded
30 ml/2 tbsp sunflower oil
5 ml/1 tsp cumin seeds
150 g/5 oz/¾ cup red lentils
250 ml/8 fl oz/1 cup water
15 ml/1 tbsp hot curry paste
200 ml/7 fl oz/scant 1 cup
   coconut cream
juice of 1 lemon
handful of fresh coriander leaves
25 g/1 oz/¼ cup flaked almonds
salt and pepper

VARIATION
Try making this dhal with yellow split peas: they take longer to cook and a little extra water has to be added but the result is equally tasty.

root ginger   *onion*   *garlic*

cumin seeds   *sunflower oil*   *red chillies*

red lentils

curry paste

coconut cream   *lemon juice*

coriander   *flaked almonds*

1 Use a vegetable peeler to peel the ginger and finely chop it with the onion, garlic and chillies.

2 Heat the oil in a large shallow saucepan. Add the ginger, onion, garlic, chillies and cumin. Cook for 5 minutes, until softened but not coloured.

3 Stir the lentils, water and curry paste into the pan. Bring to the boil, cover and cook gently over a low heat for 15–20 minutes, stirring occasionally, until the lentils are just tender and not yet broken.

4 Stir in all but 30 ml/2 tbsp of the coconut cream. Bring to the boil and cook, uncovered, for a further 15–20 minutes, until the mixture is thick and pulpy. Remove from the heat, then stir in the lemon juice and the whole coriander leaves. Add salt and pepper to taste.

5 Heat a large frying pan and cook the flaked almonds for one or two minutes on each side until golden brown. Stir about three-quarters of the toasted almonds into the dhal.

6 Transfer the dhal to a serving bowl and swirl in the remaining coconut cream. Scatter the reserved almonds on top and serve warm.

Sweet Pepper Salsa

Roasting peppers enhances their flavour and gives them a soft texture – the perfect preparation for salsas. Serve with poached salmon.

Serves 4

INGREDIENTS
1 red pepper
1 yellow pepper
5 ml/1 tsp cumin seeds
1 red chilli, seeded
30 ml/2 tbsp chopped fresh
   coriander leaves
30 ml/2 tbsp olive oil
15 ml/1 tbsp red wine vinegar
salt and pepper

yellow pepper

red pepper

red chilli

coriander

cumin seeds

olive oil

red wine vinegar

1 Preheat the grill to medium. Place the peppers on a baking sheet and grill them for 8–10 minutes, turning regularly, until their skins have blackened and are blistered.

2 Place the peppers in a bowl and cover with a clean dish towel. Leave for 5 minutes so the steam helps to lift the skin away from the flesh.

3 Meanwhile, place the cumin seeds in a small frying pan. Heat gently, stirring, until the seeds start to splutter and release their aroma. Remove the pan from the heat, then tip out the seeds into a mortar and crush them lightly with a pestle.

4 When the peppers are cool enough to handle, pierce a hole in the bottom of each and squeeze out all of the juices into a bowl.

5 Peel and core the peppers, discarding the seeds, then process the flesh in a blender or food processor with the chilli and coriander until finely chopped.

6 Stir in the oil, vinegar and cumin with salt and pepper to taste. Serve at room temperature.

COOK'S TIP

Choose red, yellow or orange peppers for this salsa as the green variety is less sweet.

Cannellini Bean Dip

This soft bean dip or pâté is good spread on wheaten crackers or toasted muffins. Alternatively, it can be served with wedges of tomato and a crisp green salad.

Serves 4

INGREDIENTS
400 g/14 oz can cannellini beans
grated rind and juice of 1 lemon
30 ml/2 tbsp olive oil
1 garlic clove, finely chopped
30 ml/2 tbsp chopped fresh parsley
red Tabasco sauce, to taste
cayenne pepper
salt and pepper

Very nice lemon & parsley come through great.

cannellini beans

olive oil

lemon juice and rind

garlic

parsley

red Tabasco sauce

cayenne pepper

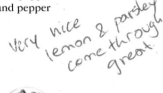

1 Drain the beans in a sieve and rinse them well under cold water. Transfer to a shallow bowl.

2 Use a potato masher to roughly purée the beans, then stir in the lemon and olive oil.

3 Stir in the chopped garlic and parsley. Add Tabasco sauce and salt and pepper to taste.

4 Spoon the mixture into a small bowl and dust lightly with cayenne pepper. Chill until ready to serve.

VARIATION

Other beans can be used for this dip, for example butter beans or kidney beans.

Coriander Pesto Salsa

This aromatic salsa is delicious drizzled over fish and chicken, tossed with pasta ribbons or used to dress a fresh avocado and tomato salad. To transform it into a dip, mix it with a little mayonnaise or soured cream.

Serves 4

INGREDIENTS
50 g/2 oz fresh coriander leaves
15 g/½ oz fresh parsley
2 red chillies
1 garlic clove
50 g/2 oz/⅓ cup shelled
  pistachio nuts
25 g/1 oz Parmesan cheese,
  finely grated
90 ml/6 tbsp olive oil
juice of 2 limes
salt and pepper

coriander   parsley

garlic   pistachio nuts   red chillies

olive oil   Parmesan cheese   lime juice

VARIATION

Any number of different herbs or nuts may be used to make a similar salsa to this one – try a mixture of rosemary and parsley, or add a handful of black olives.

1 Process the fresh coriander and parsley in a blender or food processor until finely chopped.

2 Halve the chillies lengthways and remove their seeds. Add to the herbs together with the garlic and process until finely chopped.

3 Add the pistachio nuts to the herb mixture and pulse the power until they are roughly chopped. Stir in the Parmesan cheese, olive oil and lime juice.

4 Add salt and pepper, to taste. Spoon the mixture into a serving bowl and cover and chill until ready to serve.

Butternut Squash and Parmesan Dip

Butternut squash has a rich, nutty flavour and tastes especially good roasted. Serve this dip with melba toast or cheese straws.

Serves 4

INGREDIENTS
1 butternut squash
15 g/½ oz/1 tbsp butter
4 garlic cloves, unpeeled
30 ml/2 tbsp freshly grated
  Parmesan cheese
45–75 ml/3–5 tbsp double cream
salt and pepper

butternut squash

garlic

butter

Parmesan cheese

double cream

COOK'S TIP
If you don't have a blender or food processor, simply mash the squash in a bowl using a potato masher, then beat in the grated cheese and cream using a wooden spoon.

1 Preheat the oven to 200°C/400°F/ Gas 6. Halve the butternut squash lengthways, then scoop out and discard the seeds.

2 Use a small, sharp knife to deeply score the flesh in a criss-cross pattern: cut as close to the skin as possible, but take care not to cut through it.

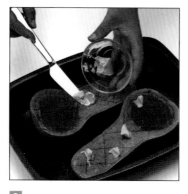

3 Arrange both halves in a small roasting tin and dot them with the butter. Sprinkle with salt and pepper and roast for 20 minutes.

4 Tuck the unpeeled garlic cloves around the squash in the roasting tin and continue baking for 20 minutes, until the butternut squash is tender and softened.

5 Scoop the flesh out of the squash shells and place it in a blender or food processor. Slip the garlic cloves out of their skins and add to the squash. Process until smooth.

VARIATION
Try making this dip with pumpkin or other types of squash, such as acorn squash or New Zealand kabocha.

6 With the motor running, add all but 15 ml/1 tsp of the Parmesan cheese and then the cream. Check the seasoning and spoon the dip into a serving bowl: it is at its best served warm. Scatter the reserved cheese over the dip.

Blue Cheese Dip

This dip can be mixed up in next-to-no-time and is delicious served with pears. Add more yogurt to make a great dressing.

Serves 4

INGREDIENTS
150 g/5 oz blue cheese, such as
   Stilton or Danish Blue
150 g/5oz/⅔ cup soft cheese
75 ml/5 tbsp Greek-style yogurt
salt and pepper

*blue
cheese*

*soft
cheese*

*Greek-style
yogurt*

1 Crumble the blue cheese into a bowl. Using a wooden spoon, beat the cheese to soften it.

2 Add the soft cheese and beat well to blend the two cheeses together.

3 Gradually beat in the Greek-style yogurt, adding enough to give you the consistency you prefer.

4 Season with lots of black pepper and a little salt. Chill until ready to serve.

COOK'S TIP
This is a very thick dip to which you can add a little more Greek-style yogurt, or stir in a little milk, for a softer consistency.

Red Onion Raita

Raita is a traditional Indian accompaniment for hot curries. It is also delicious served with poppadoms as a dip.

Serves 4

INGREDIENTS

5 ml/1 tsp cumin seeds
1 small garlic clove
1 small green chilli, seeded
1 large red onion
150 ml/¼ pint/⅔ cup natural
 yogurt
30 ml/2 tbsp chopped fresh
 coriander, plus extra, to garnish
2.5 ml/½ tsp sugar
salt

cumin   garlic   green
                    chilli

red onion   coriander

yogurt   sugar

1 Heat a small pan and dry-fry the cumin seeds for 1–2 minutes, until they release their aroma and begin to pop.

2 Lightly crush the seeds in a pestle and mortar or flatten them with the heel of a heavy-bladed knife.

3 Finely chop the garlic, chilli and red onion. Stir into the yogurt with the crushed cumin seeds and coriander.

4 Add sugar and salt to taste. Spoon the raita into a small bowl and chill until ready to serve. Garnish with extra coriander before serving.

COOK'S TIP

For an extra tangy raita stir in 15 ml/1 tbsp lemon juice. To make a pretty garnish, reserve a few thin wedges of onion, before chopping the rest.

Mellow Garlic Dip

Two whole heads of garlic may seem like a lot but, once cooked, it becomes sweet and mellow. Serve with crunchy bread sticks and crisps.

Serves 4

INGREDIENTS
2 whole garlic heads
15 ml/1 tbsp olive oil
60 ml/4 tbsp mayonnaise
75 ml/5 tbsp Greek-style yogurt
5 ml/1 tsp wholegrain mustard
salt and pepper

garlic

olive oil

mayonnaise

Greek-style yogurt

wholegrain mustard

1 Preheat the oven to 200°C/400°F/Gas 6. Separate the garlic cloves and place them in a small roasting tin.

3 Trim off the root end of each roasted garlic clove. Peel the cloves and discard the skins.

2 Pour the olive oil over the garlic cloves and turn them with a spoon to coat them evenly. Roast for 20–30 minutes, until the garlic is tender and softened. Leave to cool for 5 minutes.

4 Place the roasted garlic on a chopping board and sprinkle with salt. Mash with a fork until puréed.

5 Place the garlic in a small bowl and stir in the mayonnaise, yogurt and wholegrain mustard.

COOK'S TIP
If you are already cooking on a barbecue, leave the garlic heads whole and cook them on the hot barbecue until tender, then peel and mash.

VARIATION

For a low fat version of this dip, use reduced-fat mayonnaise and low fat natural yogurt.

6 Check and adjust the seasoning, then spoon the dip into a bowl. Cover and chill until ready to serve.

Tsatziki

Serve this classic Greek dip with strips of toasted pitta bread.

Serves 4

INGREDIENTS
1 mini cucumber
4 spring onions
1 garlic clove
200 ml/7 fl oz/scant 1 cup Greek-style yogurt
45 ml/3 tbsp chopped fresh mint
fresh mint sprig, to garnish (optional)
salt and pepper

mini cucumber

spring onions

garlic

Greek-style yogurt

mint

COOK'S TIP
Choose Greek-style yogurt for this dip – it has a higher fat content than most yogurts, which gives it a deliciously rich, creamy texture.

1 Trim the ends from the cucumber, then cut it into 5 mm/¼ in dice.

2 Trim the spring onions and garlic, then chop both very finely.

3 Beat the yogurt until smooth, if necessary, then gently stir in the cucumber, onions, garlic and mint.

4 Transfer the mixture to a serving bowl and add salt and plenty of freshly ground black pepper to taste. Chill until ready to serve and then garnish with a small mint sprig, if you like.

Soured Cream Cooler

This cooling dip is a perfect accompaniment to hot and spicy Mexican dishes. Alternatively, serve it as a snack with the fieriest tortilla chips you can find.

Serves 2

INGREDIENTS
1 small yellow pepper
2 small tomatoes
30 ml/2 tbsp chopped fresh parsley
150 ml/¼ pint/⅔ cup soured
  cream
grated lemon rind, to garnish

yellow pepper

tomatoes

parsley

soured cream

lemon rind

1 Halve the pepper lengthways. Remove the core and seeds, then cut the flesh into tiny dice.

2 Halve the tomatoes, then scoop out and discard the seeds and cut the flesh into tiny dice.

3 Stir the pepper and tomato dice and the chopped parsley into the soured cream and mix well.

4 Spoon the dip into a small bowl and chill. Garnish with grated lemon rind before serving.

VARIATION
Use finely diced avocado or cucumber in place of the pepper or tomato.

Creamy Aubergine Dip

Spread this velvet-textured dip thickly on to toasted rounds of bread, then top them with slivers of sun-dried tomato to make wonderful, Italian-style crostini.

Serves 4

INGREDIENTS
1 large aubergine
1 small onion
2 garlic cloves
30 ml/2 tbsp olive oil
60 ml/4 tbsp chopped fresh parsley
75 ml/5 tbsp crème fraîche
red Tabasco sauce, to taste
juice of 1 lemon, to taste
salt and pepper

aubergine

garlic

onion

olive oil

parsley

crème fraîche

red Tabasco sauce

lemon juice

1 Preheat the grill to medium. Place the whole aubergine on a baking sheet and grill it for 20–30 minutes, turning occasionally, until the skin is blackened and wrinkled, and the aubergine feels soft when squeezed.

2 Cover the aubergine with a clean dish towel and leave it to cool for about 5 minutes.

3 Finely chop the onion and garlic. Heat the oil in a frying pan and cook the onion and garlic for 5 minutes, until softened, but not browned.

4 Peel the skin from the aubergine. Mash the flesh with a large fork or potato masher to make a pulpy purée.

5 Stir in the onion and garlic, parsley and crème fraîche. Add Tabasco, lemon juice and salt and pepper to taste.

6 Transfer the dip to a serving bowl and serve warm or leave to cool and serve at room temperature.

COOK'S TIP
The aubergine can be roasted in the oven at 200°C/400°F/Gas 6 for 20 minutes, if preferred.

Thai Red Curry Sauce

Serve this with mini spring rolls or spicy Indonesian crackers, or toss it into freshly cooked rice noodles for a delicious main-meal accompaniment.

Serves 4

INGREDIENTS
200 ml/7 fl oz/scant 1 cup coconut cream
10–15 ml/2–3 tsp Thai red curry paste
4 spring onions, plus extra, to garnish
30 ml/2 tbsp chopped fresh coriander
1 red chilli, seeded and thinly sliced into rings
5 ml/1 tsp soy sauce
juice of 1 lime
sugar, to taste
25 g/1 oz/¼ cup dry-roasted peanuts
salt and pepper

coconut cream

Thai red curry paste

spring onions

soy sauce

red chilli

coriander

lime juice

sugar

dry-roasted peanuts

1 Pour the coconut cream into a small bowl and stir in the curry paste.

2 Trim and finely slice the spring onions diagonally. Stir into the coconut cream with the coriander and chilli.

COOK'S TIP
The dip may be prepared in advance up to the end of step 3. Sprinkle the peanuts over just before serving.

3 Stir in the soy sauce, lime juice, sugar, salt and pepper to taste. Pour the sauce into a small serving bowl.

4 Finely chop the dry-roasted peanuts and sprinkle them over the sauce. Serve immediately. Garnish with spring onions sliced lengthways.

Fat-free Saffron Dip

Serve this mild dip with fresh vegetable crudités - it is particularly good with florets of cauliflower.

Serves 4

INGREDIENTS
15 ml/1 tbsp boiling water
small pinch of saffron strands
200 g/7 oz/scant 1 cup fat-free
    fromage frais
10 fresh chives
10 fresh basil leaves
salt and pepper

saffron strands   *fromage frais*

chives   *basil leaves*

1 Pour the boiling water into a small container and add the saffron strands. Leave to infuse for 3 minutes.

2 Beat the fromage frais until smooth, then stir in the infused saffron liquid.

3 Use a pair of scissors to snip the chives into the dip. Tear the basil leaves into small pieces and stir them in.

4 Add salt and pepper to taste. Serve immediately.

VARIATION

Leave out the saffron and add a squeeze of lemon or lime juice instead.

61

Thousand Island Dip

This variation on the classic Thousand Island dressing is far removed from the original version, but can be served in the same way – with grilled king prawns laced on to bamboo skewers for dipping or with a simple mixed seafood salad.

VARIATION
Stir in cayenne pepper or a chopped fresh chilli for a more fiery dip.

Serves 4

INGREDIENTS
4 sun-dried tomatoes in oil
4 tomatoes
150 g/5 oz/⅔ cup soft cheese
60 ml/4 tbsp mayonnaise
30 ml/2 tbsp tomato purée
30 ml/2 tbsp chopped fresh parsley
grated rind and juice of 1 lemon
red Tabasco sauce, to taste
5 ml/1 tsp Worcestershire or soy
    sauce
salt and pepper

sun-dried
tomatoes
in oil

soft
cheese

tomatoes

parsley

mayonnaise

tomato
purée

Worcestershire
sauce

red
Tabasco
sauce

lemon juice
and rind

1 Drain the sun-dried tomatoes on kitchen paper to remove excess oil, then finely chop them.

2 Skewer each tomato in turn on a metal fork and hold in a gas flame for 1–2 minutes, until the skin wrinkles and splits. Slip off and discard the skins, then halve the tomatoes and scoop out the seeds with a teaspoon. Finely chop the tomato flesh.

3 Beat the soft cheese, then gradually beat in the mayonnaise and tomato purée.

4 Stir in the chopped parsley and sun-dried tomatoes, then add the chopped tomatoes and their seeds and mix well.

5 Add the lemon rind and juice and Tabasco to taste. Stir in Worcestershire or soy sauce, and salt and pepper.

6 Transfer the dip to a bowl, cover and chill until ready to serve.

Chilli Relish

This spicy relish will keep for at least a week in the fridge. Serve it with bangers and burgers.

Serves 8

INGREDIENTS
6 tomatoes
1 onion
1 red pepper, seeded
2 garlic cloves
30 ml/2 tbsp olive oil
5 ml/1 tsp ground cinnamon
5 ml/1 tsp chilli flakes
5 ml/1 tsp ground ginger
5 ml/1 tsp salt
2.5 ml/½ tsp freshly ground
   black pepper
75 g/3 oz/⅓ cup light muscovado
   sugar
75 ml/5 tbsp cider vinegar
handful of fresh basil leaves

tomatoes

onion

garlic

red pepper

olive oil

ground
cinnamon

chilli flakes

muscovado sugar

ground
ginger

cider vinegar

basil

COOK'S TIP
This relish thickens slightly on cooling so do not worry if the mixture seems a little wet at the end of step 5.

1 Skewer each of the tomatoes in turn on a metal fork and hold in a gas flame for 1–2 minutes, turning until the skin splits and wrinkles. Slip off the skins, then roughly chop the tomatoes.

2 Roughly chop the onion, red pepper and garlic. Heat the oil in a saucepan. Add the onion, red pepper and garlic to the pan.

3 Cook gently for 5–8 minutes, until the pepper is softened. Add the chopped tomatoes, cover and cook for 5 minutes, until the tomatoes release their juices.

4 Stir in the cinnamon, chilli flakes, ginger, salt, pepper, sugar and vinegar. Bring gently to the boil, stirring until the sugar dissolves.

5 Simmer, uncovered, for 20 minutes, until the mixture is pulpy. Stir in the basil leaves and check the seasoning.

6 Allow to cool completely then transfer to a glass jar or a plastic container with a tightly fitting lid. Store, covered, in the fridge.

Oriental Hoisin Dip

This speedy Oriental dip needs no cooking and can be made in just a few minutes – it tastes great with mini spring rolls or prawn crackers.

Serves 4

INGREDIENTS
4 spring onions
4 cm/1½ in piece root ginger
2 red chillies
2 garlic cloves
60 ml/4 tbsp hoisin sauce
120 ml/4 fl oz/½ cup passata
5 ml/1 tsp sesame oil (optional)

onions

root ginger

garlic

red
chillies

sesame oil

hoisin sauce

passata

1 Trim off and discard the green ends of the spring onions. Slice the remainder very thinly.

2 Peel the ginger with a swivel-bladed vegetable peeler, then chop it finely.

3 Halve the chillies lengthways and remove their seeds. Finely slice the flesh widthways into tiny strips. Finely chop the garlic.

4 Stir together the hoisin sauce, passata, spring onions, ginger, chilli, garlic and sesame oil, if using, and serve within 1 hour.

COOK'S TIP
Hoisin sauce makes an excellent base for full-flavour dips, especially when combining crunchy vegetables and other Oriental seasonings.

Smoky Tomato Salsa

The smoky flavour in this recipe comes from both the smoked bacon and the commercial liquid smoke marinade. Served with soured cream, this salsa makes a great baked potato filler.

Serves 4

INGREDIENTS
450 g/1 lb tomatoes
4 rashers smoked streaky bacon
15 ml/1 tbsp vegetable oil
45 ml/3 tbsp chopped fresh
   coriander leaves or parsley
1 garlic clove, finely chopped
15 ml/1 tbsp liquid smoke marinade
juice of 1 lime
salt and pepper

tomatoes
vegetable oil
coriander
smoked streaky bacon
garlic
lime juice
liquid smoke

1 Skewer the tomatoes on a metal fork and hold them in a gas flame for 1–2 minutes, turning until their skins split and wrinkle. Slip off the skins, halve, scoop out and discard the seeds, then finely dice the tomato flesh.

2 Cut the bacon into small strips. Heat the oil in a frying pan and cook the bacon for 5 minutes, stirring occasionally, until crisp and browned. Remove from the heat and allow to cool for a few minutes.

3 Mix the tomatoes, bacon, coriander or parsley, garlic, liquid smoke, lime juice and salt and pepper to taste.

4 Transfer to a serving bowl and chill until ready to serve.

VARIATION
Give this smoky salsa an extra kick by adding a dash of Tabasco or a pinch of dried chilli flakes.

Sweet Mango Relish

Stir a spoonful of this relish into soups and stews for added flavour or serve it with a wedge of Cheddar cheese and chunks of crusty bread.

VARIATION
Select alternative spices to suit your own taste: for example, add juniper berries in place of the star anise or try cumin seeds.

Makes 750 ml/1¼ pints/ 3 cups

INGREDIENTS

2 large mangoes
1 cooking apple
2 shallots
4 cm/1½ in piece root ginger
2 garlic cloves
115 g/4 oz/cup small sultanas
2 star anise
5 ml/1 tsp ground cinnamon
2.5 ml/½ tsp dried chilli flakes
2.5 ml/½ tsp salt
175 ml/6 fl oz/¾ cup cider vinegar
130 g/3½ oz/scant ½ cup light
    muscovado sugar

mangoes

cooking apple

shallots

root ginger

garlic

star anise

sultanas

ground cinnamon

chilli flakes

cider vinegar

muscovado sugar

1 Hold the mangoes, one at a time, upright on a chopping board and use a large knife to slice the flesh away from either side of the large flat stone in two portions. Using a smaller knife, carefully trim away any flesh still clinging to the top and bottom of the stone.

2 Score the flesh of the mango halves deeply, taking care to avoid cutting through the skin: make parallel incisions about 1 cm/½ in apart; turn and cut lines in the opposite direction. Carefully turn the skin inside out so the flesh stands out like hedgehog spikes. Slice the dice away from the skin.

3 Using a sharp knife, peel and roughly chop the apple, shallots, ginger and garlic.

4 Place the mango, apple, shallots, ginger, garlic and sultanas in a large pan. Add the spices, salt, vinegar and sugar.

5 Bring to the boil, stirring until the sugar dissolves. Reduce the heat and simmer gently for 45 minutes, stirring occasionally, until the chutney has reduced and thickened.

6 Allow the chutney to cool for about 5 minutes, then pot it into clean jars. Cool completely, cover and store in the fridge for up to 2 months.

Spicy Sweetcorn Relish

Serve this simple spicy relish with Red Onion
Raita, Sweet Mango Relish and a plateful of
crisp onion bhajis for a fabulous Indian-
style starter.

Serves 4

INGREDIENTS
1 large onion
1 red chilli, seeded
2 garlic cloves
30 ml/2 tbsp vegetable oil
5 ml/1 tsp black mustard seeds
10 ml/2 tsp hot curry powder
320 g/11¼ oz can sweetcorn
grated rind and juice of 1 lime
45 ml/3 tbsp chopped fresh
   coriander
salt and pepper

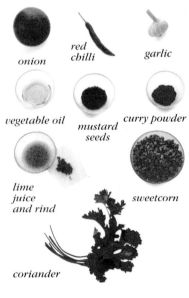

onion   red chilli   garlic

vegetable oil   mustard seeds   curry powder

lime juice and rind   sweetcorn

coriander

COOK'S TIP
Opt for canned rather than
frozen sweetcorn if possible as
the kernels are plump, moist
and ready to eat.

1 Chop the onion, chilli and garlic.
Heat the oil in a large frying pan and
cook the onion, chilli and garlic over a
high heat for 5 minutes, until the onions
are just beginning to brown.

2 Stir in the mustard seeds and curry
powder, then cook for a further
2 minutes, stirring, until the seeds start to
splutter and the onions are browned.

3 Remove the fried onion mixture
from the heat and allow to cool. Place in
a glass bowl. Drain the sweetcorn and
stir into the onion mixture.

4 Add the lime rind and juice,
coriander and salt and pepper to taste.
Cover and serve at room temperature.

Toffee Onion Relish

Slow, gentle cooking reduces the onions to a soft, caramelised relish in this recipe.

Serves 4

INGREDIENTS
3 large onions
50 g/2 oz/4 tbsp butter
30 ml/2 tbsp olive oil
30 ml/2 tbsp light muscovado sugar
30 ml/2 tbsp pickled capers
30 ml/2 tbsp chopped fresh parsley
salt and pepper

onions

olive oil

muscovado
sugar

butter

capers

parsley

1 Peel the onions and halve them vertically, through the core, then slice them thinly.

2 Heat the butter and oil together in a large saucepan. Add the onions and sugar and cook very gently for 30 minutes over a low heat, stirring occasionally, until reduced to a soft rich brown toffeed mixture.

3 Roughly chop the capers and stir into the toffee onions. Allow to cool completely.

4 Stir in the chopped parsley and add salt and pepper to taste. Cover and chill until ready to serve.

VARIATION

Try making this recipe with red onions or shallots for a subtle variation in flavour.

Barbecued Sweetcorn Salsa

Serve this succulent salsa with smoked meats or a juicy grilled gammon steak.

Serves 4

INGREDIENTS
2 corn cobs
30 ml/2 tbsp melted butter
4 tomatoes
6 spring onions
1 garlic clove
30 ml/2 tbsp fresh lemon juice
30 ml/2 tbsp olive oil
red Tabasco sauce, to taste
salt and pepper

corn cobs

butter

tomatoes

spring onions

garlic

lemon juice

olive oil

red Tabasco sauce

1 Remove the husks and silky threads covering the corn cobs. Brush the cobs with the melted butter and gently barbecue or grill them for 20–30 minutes, turning occasionally, until tender and tinged brown.

2 To remove the kernels, stand the cob upright on a chopping board and use a large, heavy knife to slice down the length of the cob.

3 Skewer the tomatoes in turn on a metal fork and hold in a gas flame for 1–2 minutes, turning until the skin splits and wrinkles. Slip off the skin and dice the tomato flesh.

4 Finely chop the spring onions and garlic, then mix with the corn and tomato in a small bowl.

5 Stir the lemon juice and olive oil together, adding Tabasco, salt and pepper to taste.

6 Pour this over the salsa and stir well. Cover the salsa and leave to infuse at room temperature for 1–2 hours before serving.

Plantain Salsa

Here is a summery salsa, that is perfect for lazy outdoor eating. Serve with salted potato crisps for dipping.

Serves 4

INGREDIENTS
knob of butter
4 ripe plantains
handful of fresh coriander, plus
    extra, to garnish
30 ml/2 tbsp olive oil
5 ml/1 tsp cayenne pepper
salt and pepper

plantains

butter   *coriander*

olive oil

cayenne pepper

1 Preheat the oven to 200°C/400°F/Gas 6. Grease four pieces of foil with the knob of butter.

2 Peel the plantains and place one on each piece of foil. Fold the foil over tightly to form a parcel.

3 Bake the plantain for 25 minutes, until tender. Alternatively, the plantain may be cooked in the embers of a charcoal barbecue.

4 Allow the parcels to cool slightly, then remove the plantains, discarding any liquid, and place in a blender or food processor.

5 Process the plantains with the coriander until fairly smooth. Stir in the olive oil, cayenne pepper and salt and pepper to taste.

6 Serve immediately as the salsa will discolour and over-thicken if left to cool for too long. Garnish with torn coriander leaves.

COOK'S TIP
Be sure to choose ripe plantains with blackened skins for this recipe as they will be at their sweetest and tenderest.

Tart Tomato Relish

The whole lime used in this recipe adds a pleasantly sour after-taste. Serve with grilled or roast pork or lamb.

Serves 4

INGREDIENTS

2 pieces stem ginger
1 lime
450 g/1 lb cherry tomatoes
115 g/4 oz/½ cup dark muscovado
    sugar
100 ml/3½ fl oz/scant ½ cup white
    wine vinegar
5 ml/1 tsp salt

stem
ginger

cherry
tomatoes

muscovado
sugar

white wine
vinegar

lime

VARIATION
If preferred, use ordinary tomatoes, roughly chopped, in place of the cherry tomatoes.

1 Coarsely chop the ginger. Slice the whole lime thinly, then chop it into small pieces; do not remove the rind.

2 Place the whole tomatoes, sugar, vinegar, salt, ginger and lime together in a saucepan.

3 Bring to the boil, stirring until the sugar dissolves, then simmer rapidly for 45 minutes. Stir regularly until the liquid has evaporated and the relish is thickened and pulpy.

4 Allow the relish to cool for about 5 minutes, then spoon it into clean jars. Cool completely, cover and store in the fridge for up to 1 month.

Spiced Carrot Dip

This is a delicious low-fat dip with a sweet and spicy flavour. Serve wheat crackers or fiery tortilla chips as accompaniments for dipping.

Serves 4

INGREDIENTS
1 onion
3 carrots, plus extra, to garnish
grated rind and juice of 2 oranges
15 ml/1 tbsp hot curry paste
150 ml/¼ pint/⅔ cup low-fat
   natural yogurt
handful of fresh basil leaves
15–30 ml/1–2 tbsp fresh lemon
   juice, to taste
red Tabasco sauce, to taste
salt and pepper

onion

carrots

orange rind and juice

curry paste

basil

lemon juice

low fat natural yogurt

red Tabasco sauce

1 Finely chop the onion. Peel and grate the carrots. Place the onion, carrots, orange rind and juice and curry paste in a small saucepan. Bring to the boil, cover and simmer for 10 minutes, until tender.

2 Process the mixture in a blender or food processor until smooth. Leave to cool completely.

VARIATION
Greek-style yogurt or soured cream may be used in place of the natural yogurt to make a richer, creamy dip.

3 Stir in the yogurt, then tear the basil leaves into small pieces and stir them into the carrot mixture.

4 Add the lemon juice, Tabasco, salt and pepper to taste. Serve within a few hours at room temperature. Garnish with grated carrot.

Tomato and Orange Pepper Salsa

Serve this sunny salsa with spicy sausages or grilled meats.

Serves 4

INGREDIENTS
4 tomatoes
1 orange pepper
4 spring onions, plus extra, to garnish
handful of fresh coriander leaves
juice of 1 lime
salt and pepper

tomatoes

orange pepper

*spring
onions*

coriander

lime juice

1 Halve the tomatoes. Scoop out the seeds with a teaspoon and discard. Finely chop the flesh.

2 Spear the pepper on a metal fork and turn it in a gas flame for 1–2 minutes until the skin blisters and chars.

3 Peel off and discard the skin. Remove the core and scrape out the seeds. Finely chop the flesh.

4 Finely chop the spring onions and coriander, then mix both with the pepper and tomato flesh.

5 Squeeze over the lime juice and add salt and pepper to taste. Toss well to mix.

6 Transfer the salsa to a bowl and chill until ready to serve. Garnish with shreds of spring onion.

VARIATION

Try using a selection of tomatoes, such as plum or cherry, for a variety of textures and flavours.

Fresh Tomato and Tarragon Salsa

Plum tomatoes, garlic, olive oil and balsamic vinegar make for a very Mediterranean salsa – try serving this with grilled lamb cutlets or toss it with freshly cooked pasta.

Serves 4

INGREDIENTS
8 plum tomatoes
1 small garlic clove
60 ml/4 tbsp olive oil
15 ml/1 tbsp balsamic vinegar
30 ml/2 tbsp chopped fresh
   tarragon, plus extra, to garnish
salt and pepper

plum tomatoes   *garlic*

olive oil   *balsamic vinegar*

tarragon

COOK'S TIP
Be sure to serve this salsa at room temperature as the tomatoes taste less sweet, and rather acidic, when chilled.

1 Skewer the tomatoes in turn on a metal fork and hold in a gas flame for 1–2 minutes, turning until the skin splits and wrinkles.

2 Slip off the skins and finely chop the tomato flesh.

3 Using a sharp knife, crush or finely chop the garlic.

4 Whisk together the olive oil, balsamic vinegar and plenty of salt and pepper.

5 Finely chop the tarragon and stir it into the olive oil mixture.

6 Mix the tomatoes and garlic in a bowl and pour the tarragon dressing over. Leave to infuse for at least 1 hour before serving at room temperature. Garnish with shredded tarragon leaves.

Orange and Chive Salsa

Fresh chives and sweet oranges provide a very
cheerful combination of flavours.

Serves 4

INGREDIENTS
2 large oranges
1 beefsteak tomato
bunch of chives
1 garlic clove
30 ml/2 tbsp olive oil
sea salt

oranges

beefsteak
tomato

garlic

chives

olive oil

1 Slice the bottom off the orange so
that it will stand firmly on a chopping
board. Using a large sharp knife, remove
the peel by slicing from the top to the
bottom of the orange.

2 Hold the orange in one hand over a
bowl. Slice towards the middle of the
fruit, to one side of a segment, and then
gently twist the knife to ease the
segment away from the membrane and
out of the orange. Repeat to remove all
the segments. Squeeze any juice from
the remaining membrane. Prepare the
second orange in the same way.

3 Roughly chop the orange segments
and place them in the bowl with the
collected juice.

4 Halve the tomato and use a
teaspoon to scoop the seeds into the
bowl. Finely dice the flesh and add to the
oranges in the bowl.

5 Hold the bunch of chives neatly
together and use a pair of kitchen
scissors to snip them into the bowl.

6 Thinly slice the garlic and stir it into
the orange mixture. Pour over the olive
oil, season with sea salt and stir well to
mix. Serve within 2 hours.

VARIATION
Add a little diced mozzarella
cheese to make a more
substantial salsa.

Aromatic Peach and Cucumber Salsa

Angostura bitters add an unusual and very pleasing flavour to this salsa. Distinctive, sweet-tasting mint complements chicken and other main meat dishes.

Serves 4

INGREDIENTS
2 peaches
1 mini cucumber
2.5 ml/½ tsp Angostura bitters
15 ml/1 tbsp olive oil
10 ml/2 tsp fresh lemon juice
30 ml/2 tbsp chopped fresh mint
salt and pepper

peaches   *mini cucumber*

Angostura bitters   *olive oil*

lemon juice   *mint*

COOK'S TIP
The texture of the peach and the crispness of the cucumber will fade fairly rapidly, so try to prepare this salsa as close to serving time as possible.

1 Using a small sharp knife, carefully score a line right around the circumference of each peach, cutting just through the skin.

2 Bring a large pan of water to the boil. Add the peaches and blanch them for 60 seconds. Drain and briefly refresh in cold water.

3 Peel off and discard the skin. Halve the peaches and remove their stones. Finely dice the flesh and place in a bowl.

4 Trim the ends off the cucumber, then finely dice the flesh and stir it into the peaches.

5 Stir the Angostura bitters, olive oil and lemon juice together and then stir this dressing into the peach mixture.

VARIATION
Use diced mango in place of peach for an alternative.

6 Stir in the mint with salt and pepper to taste. Chill and serve within 1 hour.

Mango and Red Onion Salsa

A very simple salsa, which is livened up by the addition of passion-fruit pulp.

Serves 4

INGREDIENTS
1 large ripe mango
1 red onion
2 passion fruit
6 large fresh basil leaves
juice of 1 lime, to taste
sea salt

mango   *red onion*

passion fruit   *basil*

lime juice

VARIATION
Sweetcorn kernels are a delicious addition to this salsa.

1 Holding the mango upright on a chopping board, use a large knife to slice the flesh away from either side of the large flat stone in two portions.

2 Using a smaller knife, trim away any flesh still clinging to the top and bottom of the stone.

3 Score the flesh of the mango halves deeply, taking care to avoid cutting through the skin: make parallel incisions about 1 cm/½ in apart; turn and cut lines in the opposite direction. Carefully turn the skin inside out so the flesh stands out like hedgehog spikes. Slice the dice away from the skin.

4 Finely chop the red onion and place it in a bowl with the mango.

5 Halve the passion fruit, scoop out the seeds and pulp, and add to the mango mixture.

6 Tear the basil leaves coarsely and stir them into the salsa with lime juice and a little sea salt to taste. Serve immediately.

Pineapple and Passion Fruit Salsa

Pile this fruity dessert salsa into brandy snap baskets or meringue nests.

Serves 6

INGREDIENTS
1 small fresh pineapple
2 passion fruit
150 ml/¼ pint/⅔ cup Greek-style
 yogurt
30 ml/2 tbsp light muscovado sugar

pineapple

*passion
fruit*

*Greek-
style
yogurt*

*muscovado
sugar*

1 Cut off the top and bottom of the pineapple so that it will stand firmly on a chopping board. Using a large sharp knife, slice off the peel.

2 Use a small sharp knife to carefully cut out the eyes.

3 Slice the pineapple and use a small pastry cutter to stamp out the tough core. Finely chop the flesh.

4 Halve the passion fruit and scoop out the seeds and pulp into a bowl.

5 Stir in the chopped pineapple and yogurt. Cover and chill.

6 Stir in the sugar just before serving the salsa.

VARIATION
Lightly whipped double cream can be used instead of Greek-style yogurt.

Malted Chocolate and Banana Dip

Malted drinks and "smoothies" are all the fashion and this delectable dip is lovely served with chunks of fruit.

Serves 4

INGREDIENTS
50 g/2 oz plain chocolate
2 large ripe bananas
15 ml/1 tbsp malt extract

plain chocolate

bananas

malt extract

1 Break the chocolate into pieces and place in a small heatproof bowl. Stand the bowl over a pan of gently simmering water and stir the chocolate occasionally until it melts. Allow to cool.

2 Cut the bananas into pieces and process them until finely chopped in a blender or food processor.

3 With the motor running, pour in the malt extract, and continue processing until the mixture is thick and frothy.

4 Drizzle in the chocolate in a steady stream and process until well blended. Serve immediately.

COOK'S TIP
This smooth dip can be prepared in advance and chilled. When ready to serve, stir in some lightly whipped cream to soften and enrich the mixture.

Sweet Apple Sauce

This buttery apple sauce can be served warm or cold with roast pork or lamb.

Serves 4

INGREDIENTS
2 Bramley's Seedling cooking apples
30 ml/2 tbsp brandy
25 g/1 oz/2 tbsp butter
25 g/1 oz/2 tbsp light muscovado
  sugar

cooking apples

butter   *brandy*

muscovado sugar

1 Using a sharp knife, peel, core and finely dice the cooking apples.

2 Place the apples in a small saucepan with the brandy, butter and sugar.

3 Heat gently, stirring, until the sugar dissolves. Cover and simmer very gently for 20–25 minutes, until the apple mixture is thick and pulpy.

4 Allow to cool completely. Cover and chill for up to 5 days.

VARIATION
Stir in a handful of small, plump sultanas with the diced apple.

Papaya and Coconut Dip

Sweet and smooth papaya teams up well with
rich coconut cream to make a luscious sweet dip.

Serves 6

INGREDIENTS
2 ripe papayas
200 ml/7 fl oz/scant 1 cup
   crème fraîche
1 piece stem ginger
fresh coconut, to decorate

papayas

*crème
fraîche*

*stem
ginger*

*fresh
coconut*

1 Halve each papaya lengthways, then
scoop out and discard the seeds. Cut a
few slices and reserve for decoration.

2 Scoop out the flesh and process
it until smooth in a blender or a
food processor.

3 Stir in the crème fraîche and process
until well blended. Finely chop the stem
ginger and stir it into the mixture, then
chill until ready to serve.

4 Pierce a hole in the "eye" of the
coconut and drain off the liquid, then
break open the coconut. Hold it securely
in one hand and hit it sharply with a
hammer.

5 Remove the shell from a piece of
coconut, then snap the nut into pieces
no wider than 2 cm/¾ in.

6 Use a swivel-bladed vegetable peeler
to shave off 2 cm/¾ in lengths of
coconut. Scatter these over the dip with
the reserved papaya before serving.

COOK'S TIP
If fresh coconut is not available,
buy coconut strands and lightly
toast in a hot oven until golden.

Mixed Melon Salsa

A combination of two very different melons gives this salsa an exciting flavour and texture.

Serves 10

INGREDIENTS
1 small orange-fleshed melon, such
  as Charentais
1 large wedge watermelon
2 oranges

*Charentais
melon*

watermelon

oranges

1 Quarter the orange-fleshed melon and remove the seeds.

2 Use a large, sharp knife to cut off the skin. Dice the flesh.

3 Pick out the seeds from the watermelon then remove the skin. Dice the flesh into small chunks.

4 Use a zester to pare long strips of rind from both oranges.

5 Halve the oranges and squeeze out all their juice.

6 Mix both types of the melon and the orange rind and juice. Chill for about 30 minutes and serve.

VARIATION

Other melons can be used for this salsa. For example, try cantaloupe, Galia or Ogen.

INDEX